THE STORY OF FLIES

Books by Dorothy E. Shuttlesworth

ABC OF BUSES

THE AGE OF REPTILES

ANIMAL CAMOUFLAGE

CLEAN AIR—SPARKLING WATER

THE DOUBLEDAY FIRST GUIDE TO ROCKS

A SENSE OF WONDER: SELECTIONS FROM GREAT WRITERS ON NATURE

THE STORY OF ANTS

THE STORY OF FLIES

THE STORY OF HORSES

THE STORY OF ROCKS

THE STORY OF SPIDERS

THE STORY OF FLIES

By Dorothy E. Shuttlesworth

Illustrated by Barbara Wolff

DOUBLEDAY & COMPANY, INC., GARDEN CITY, NEW YORK

Library of Congress Catalog Card Number: 68-17817
Copyright © 1970 by Doubleday & Company, Inc.
Printed in the United States of America
First Edtion

Contents

For Gladys and Peter Zugale
good friends "for all seasons"

THE STORY OF FLIES

Merodon equestris

Tsetse

Dragonfly

Hessian fly

Introduction

Like millions of other people, you have probably been annoyed by house flies and bitten by mosquitoes. If so, you are already acquainted with the two best-known members of the group of insects known as Diptera—the two-winged flies.

According to scientists, any insect that has only one pair of wings is a fly.

Most fiercely biting and bloodsucking insects are flies, and great is the annoyance, pain, and misery they cause. The best thing that can be said about most flies is that they are a nuisance. But many are something more. They are carriers of disease.

Of all man's insect enemies none is more dangerous or has caused more harm than the fly we commonly call a mosquito. The name, by the way, is Spanish for "little fly." Malaria is the dread disease most often associated with mosquitoes. Since the beginning of man's history this disease has caused more deaths and crippled more people than all wars put together. So serious is malaria some medical authorities claim that, until the twentieth century, half of all human deaths could be traced directly or indirectly to mosquitoes.

Even the common house fly is more than just annoyance. Dwellers in filth and sharers of man's food, house flies can and do carry diseases, particularly stomach and intestinal upsets that are often serious enough to kill babies and young children. Diarrhea, dysentery, typhoid fever, and even polio have been spread by house flies.

Then there are horse flies, deer flies, sand flies, and tsetse flies, bloodsuckers every one. They can transmit disease to man or animals when they bite. From horses and cattle to deer and kangaroos there are few animals, domestic or wild, that cannot be injured or made ill by some kind of fly.

The world's human population is "exploding"—increasing at a frightening rate—and threatens to outstrip man's food supply. Indeed, it already has in some places. Millions of people never know the comfortable feeling of being really well fed. Other millions live perpetually on the edge of starvation. Weakened by lack of food, they are easy marks for diseases of all kinds. Starvation and malnutrition may soon take over malaria's number one place as the chief killer of men. Part of the food crisis must be blamed on the many flies that destroy plants and spoil countless tons of food each year.

It would be easy to say that flies are of no use at all. Yet before man condemns them completely and decides that the best thing for the world would be to wipe them out, he should look at the other side of the picture.

While some flies destroy food, many feed on plants directly without harming them. As they flit among blossoms sucking nectar these flies carry pollen that causes the flowers to ripen into fruits and seeds. In carrying out this cross-pollination flies are second in importance only to bees. Then there are the flies that hunt and feed on other insects. They eat great quantities of the harmful plant pests. And flies are an important source of food for animals, particularly birds and fish. Without flies our world would be less beautiful and life would be less abundant. Less fun, too. Any fisherman knows that for some kinds of panfish there is no better bait than a fat white fly maggot.

The habits of many flies are little less than disgusting to human. They lay their

11

eggs on garbage, body wastes, and the decaying carcasses of dead creatures. Practically anything nasty is home for some kind of fly. The maggots eat the material in which they were hatched. Disgusting it is true, but important. Flies are scavengers, living garbage disposals. By cleaning up dead and decaying matter they perform an important task in nature.

Usually we don't think of flies as being particularly useful to scientists. Ask anyone what is the most common laboratory animal, and the answer is likely to be rats or mice. But, in terms of sheer numbers, the most common laboratory animal is a tiny fly (about 1/4 inch long) with a long name, *Drosophila melanogaster*. More commonly it is called the fruit fly.

Fruit flies have several things to recommend them. The most important of all is that they grow from egg to mature, egg-laying adult in ten days or so. Generation follows generation quickly. Thus scientists can use them to study how physical characteristics—eye color or wing shape, for example—are passed from parent to offspring through many generations. This study is the science of *genetics*. By tracing out how characteristics pass through hundreds of generations of fruit flies, scientists have worked out many laws that seem to hold true for all living things. It is safe to say that much of modern genetics is based on fruit fly experiments.

The usefulness of fruit flies as experimental animals is not limited to genetics. Scientists of the National Aeronautics and Space Administration use them in experiments to find out how living things survive in low pressure. The flies are placed in jars attached to vacuum pumps and the air is pumped out to simulate the extreme low pressures and near vacuums of outer space. Some flies have survived in pressures as low as those seventeen miles above the earth's atmosphere.

Physiology is the study of how living things operate, the chemistry and physics of life. Flies are of great value to researchers. Some are aimed at understanding the human nervous system. In other laboratories studies in muscle physiology are being carried out on fly wing muscles. The reason for this is that some flies beat their wings 200 times a second. Relatively speaking, wing muscle cells of flies are gigantic, and easy to study under microscopes.

So it turns out that the answer to "What use is a fly?" is that it depends. Some flies are helpful to us, some are harmful. But helpful or harmful, flies are important and it is necessary for us to understand them—to learn how to control those that cause misery and death, to preserve those that are helpful.

This book is about a number of flies that are important because of the trouble they cause or the good they do. In the coming chapters we will look at some of the most interesting fly families, including house flies, gnats, and mosquitoes, and their effects on man's life and work. Then in the last chapter we will find some insects that deserve attention because they are called flies even though they are not members of the Diptera group—true two-winged flies.

How to Recognize a Fly

It is believed that there are more than nine hundred thousand different kinds of insects, more than all other kinds of animals put together. Actually this number is a guess, for no one really knows how many kinds of insects there are. New ones are added to the list of recognized species each year.

Phylum, Class, Order

To make any kind of sense out of this vast number of creatures, to give each insect a name that belongs to it and no other insect, and to make sure that an insect is discovered and named only once, scientists have developed an elaborate scheme for classifying and naming them.

Every animal—not only insects—is first placed in a large group called a *phylum*. There are twenty or so such groups. Earthworms and other worms whose bodies are marked with rings belong in one phylum. Clams, oysters, scallops (the shellfish) all belong in another. Starfish, sea urchins, and other animals that have spiny or prickly skins belong in still another. All the animals in a phylum, no matter

FAMILY TREE OF INSECTS IN RELATION TO FLIES

Dobsonfly

Termite

Earwig

Grasshopper

Dragonfly

Mayfly

Wasp, ant, bee

Flea

Beetle

Moth, butterfly

Caddisfly

Fly

Bug

Sucking lice

Protura

Cicada

how different they may look, have something in common. Take for example fish, dogs, birds, and men. They all have backbones and so they belong to one phylum.

The largest phylum by far contains animals that have hard, jointed shells on the outside and several pairs of jointed legs and other appendages attached. This is the phylum Arthropoda, which means jointed-legged animals. It contains crabs, spiders, scorpions, and insects.

To keep the various kinds of animals in a phylum separate, each phylum is divided into smaller groups called *classes*. All the insects have six legs and they make up one class of the phylum Arthropoda, the class insecta as it is called. The bodies of insects are divided by clearly marked joints into three different parts: a *head* region containing the mouth and eyes; a middle part, the *thorax,* to which the legs and wings are attached; and a rear part, the *abdomen*, which contains most of the digestive and reproductive organs.

There are obvious similarities among all insects. But line up a beetle, a butterfly, a grasshopper, and a house fly side by side and you will see many obvious differences. On the basis of these differences—particularly on the number, texture,

PARTS OF A FLY

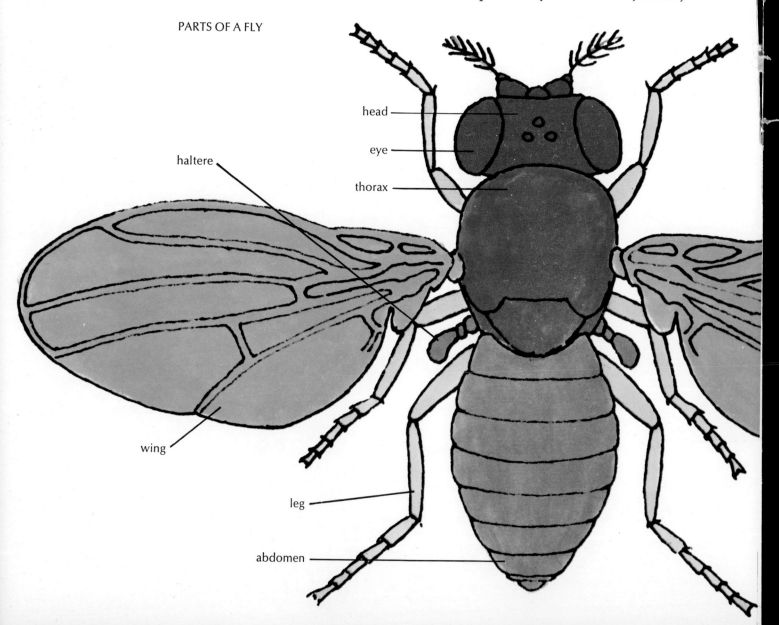

head

eye

thorax

haltere

wing

leg

abdomen

shape and function of wings—the class of insects is further divided into still smaller groups called *orders*.

House flies, horse flies, mosquitoes, and gnats have only one pair of wings and all belong to the order Diptera, from Greek words meaning two-winged. Sometimes members of the order Diptera are called "true flies" to separate them from insects such as butterflies, dragonflies, and fireflies, which, in spite of their names, have two pairs of wings.

All told, it seems there are about one hundred thousand kinds of true flies. Like the total number of insects, however, this is just a good guess. And so is the number estimated in North America, north of Mexico—seventeen thousand.

A "Typical" Fly

You can learn a lot about flies by watching a house fly, or, better yet, by trying to catch one.

An ordinary house fly is an acrobat without equal. It can walk upside down. It can zoom through the air at speeds up to several miles an hour and land suddenly and securely in almost any position.

Anyone who has ever chased a fly has marveled at its quick "takeoff" and its ability to see its pursuer even as it speeds through the air. One evening on a television show in New York City, a fly appeared on the desk of the master of ceremonies. He gave chase with a rolled-up paper and, for the next few minutes, while millions of people across the nation watched, he swatted walls and furniture in frantic pursuit. He never did hit the fly and finally gave up trying as he remarked that *nothing* was more annoying than one of these insects that seem to be smarter than people.

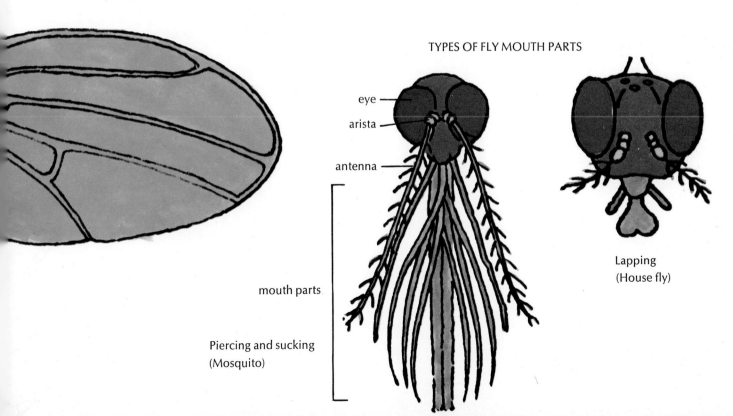

TYPES OF FLY MOUTH PARTS

eye

arista

antenna

mouth parts

Piercing and sucking
(Mosquito)

Lapping
(House fly)

A fly, of course, cannot really be considered "smart" in the ordinary sense of the word. It has no intelligence and very likely cannot learn anything. It doesn't have to, because it is so well equipped with a variety of useful organs and instincts that it can survive without learning.

Like all insects, flies have remarkable sense organs tied together by a nervous system which, while quite different from that of human beings and other animals with backbones, functions very well. It consists of a double cord of nerves running along the bottom of the insect just inside its body. The nerve cord looks something like a string of loosely strung beads. The knots or beads are swellings

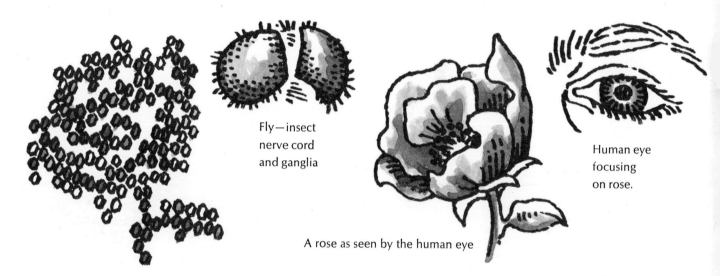

A rose as seen by a fly

Fly—insect nerve cord and ganglia

A rose as seen by the human eye

Human eye focusing on rose.

where the nerve cells are bunched together. *Ganglia* they are called, and they work like little brains to control just the part of the body in which they are located. Two large ganglia are located in the heads of flies. They are attached to the eyes and other sense organs. Other large ganglia are located in the thorax to control the wings and leg muscles. Equipped with such a nervous system specialized for quick response, remarkable powers of flight, and excellent vision, the flies we chase manage to get away more often than not.

Wings and Balancers

In the location where most other insects have a second pair of wings—attached to the thorax behind the first pair—the true flies have a pair of little knobs mounted on slender stalks. These are *halteres* or balancers. Apparently they have a great deal to do with flight, for if both halteres are removed the insect can't fly. If only one is lost, the fly swirls around aimlessly.

In flight the halteres beat very fast, and it is a good guess—supported by experiments—that they act as a stabilizer or built-in, living gyroscope. Just as the heavy,

16

spinning wheel of a toy gyroscope balances it in any position, so do the heavy—for a fly that is—knobs of the halteres keep the fly in balance.

Considering the fact that flies have only two wings, it is surprising to find that they are among the swiftest of all insects. Some flies are thought to be able to fly as fast as thirty miles per hour.

Compound Eyes

Another reason why it is so hard to swat a fly is because of its eyes. Like all insects, flies have what are known as compound eyes. If you can catch a fly without smashing it, take a look at its eyes with a magnifying glass. The eyes—which are very large in proportion to the head and may even cover most of it—are made up of many six-sided units fitted together rather like tiles in a floor. Each unit, called *a facet,* or *ommatidium,* is really a separate eye with its own lens and muscles. While the whole eye sees as many images as there are facets, all are blended together to produce a composite mosaic image.

Despite these elaborate eyes there are limitations to a fly's vision. Unlike animals with backbones, flies can neither move their eyes nor focus them. They are near-sighted. Photographs made through the lenses of compound eyes show that the sharpness of insects' vision varies from about 1/75 of that of the human eye down to about 1/1000.

But with eyes covering most of their heads and curved to receive light from almost any direction, lack of focusing power is not a serious handicap. A fly can see you from whatever direction you approach. Since your image is made up of a mosaic of little pieces, any movement quickly shifts part of the mosaic pattern and the fly responds instantly.

A close look at a fly shows that it is covered with hairs and bristles of various sorts. Some of these are sensitive to heat, some to noise, and some to sudden air currents. All give ample warning of the approaching swatter.

The one thing that makes flies such a problem to humans is that a lot of them bite and suck blood. Their mouths are made up of several jointed structures that developed from legs clustered together on the front of the head. Most typically these parts fit together to make a kind of drinking straw, as with the house flies. But just about as often the sucking mouth is equipped with a piercing beak. Mosquitoes' beaks are hair-thin and slip into human skin without pain. The bite or puncture of a horse fly feels like a jab from a large hypodermic needle.

Egg, Larva, Adult

One characteristic shared by all members of an order of insects is the way they develop from eggs into adults. True flies, the Diptera, go through four

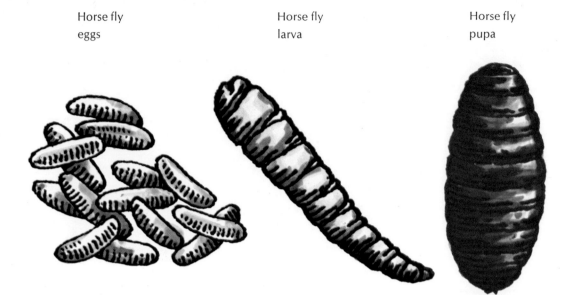

Horse fly
eggs

Horse fly
larva

Horse fly
pupa

stages in their lives. First the egg, which hatches into a worm-like creature that doesn't look anything like the adult. Newly hatched flies are called maggots, grubs, or wigglers. All can be called *larvae* (singular, *larva*), and this stage is the *larval stage*. Because their skins are fairly rigid and tough, growth requires breaking out of the old skin. When an insect sheds its skin to grow, it is said to *molt*. Only larvae can molt and only larvae can grow.

After the fly larva has popped its skin several times, getting larger with each stage, growth stops and the larval skin hardens into a tough skin. The insect is now known as a *pupa*. This is the *pupal stage* and the tough, hardened skin is called a *pupal case*. Inside a most remarkable thing takes place. The larva disintegrates, and from its cells the adult forms. When the adult is fully formed, it breaks out to feed. This is true of practically all insects.

Genus and Species

With one hundred thousand flies differing from one another in size, habits, and mouth parts, we can see that naming them calls for some further breakdown within the order Diptera. And so there is. The order is divided into *families*. The house fly, for example, belongs to the family *Muscidae*. Families are again divided into groups known as *genera*; one is called a *genus*. The house fly belongs to the genus *Musca*. But there are lots of other members of the genus, so each fly gets a further label called the *species* name. The whole scientific name of any particular fly is made by putting together the genus name and species name. This makes the house fly *Musca domestica*. Most well known of all flies, a nuisance and a pest capable of inflicting serious harm, *Musca domestica* is suitable to consider first.

18

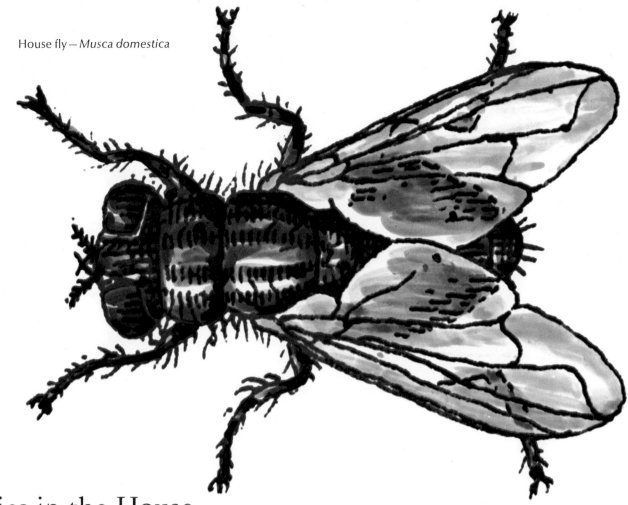

House fly — *Musca domestica*

Flies in the House

The true house fly, *Musca domestica,* is just about a half inch long. The name *domestica* is a good one for the "domestic" house fly. These insects are always closely associated with man. Three extremely unattractive characteristics make them germ carriers: their filthy habits, their huge appetites, and their ability to fly several miles, if necessary, to seek out decaying animal or vegetable matter necessary for their breeding.

On the house fly's feet are tiny pads covered with hairs from which ooze a sticky liquid. These sticky hairs help the insect to cling in any position to almost any surface. They are also responsible for bacteria sticking to the fly's feet. You can be sure that any house fly lighting on your sandwich or crawling around the sugar bowl is leaving a trail of bacteria. Fortunately most of these bacteria aren't harmful. They are usually the bacteria that cause decay. But all too often the bacteria are the germs of disease. When the wastes on which flies feed contain the germs from a sick person, the house fly carries them. There is no doubt that house flies are responsible for spreading the bacteria that cause diarrhea and dysentery. They are also known to have spread typhoid fever and have been implicated as the carriers of cholera and intestinal worms.

19

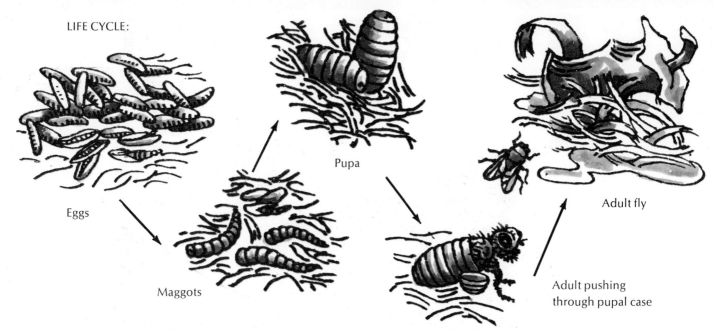

LIFE CYCLE:

Eggs

Maggots

Pupa

Adult pushing
through pupal case

Adult fly

Another way a house fly spreads infection is by vomiting on foot. It has a kind of storage stomach in which food is first stored just after eating. Later the food is regurgitated before being passed into the fly's digestive system. At that time little dabs of whatever the fly ate last may drop from its mouth and these, too, may contaminate food.

The Life Cycle

The life cycle of a house fly begins when a female lays her eggs, about a hundred at a time, in moist decaying material. The choice spots are stable manures, human feces (solid waste), and garbage of any kind. In about twelve hours, depending on the temperature, the eggs hatch into unattractive whitish larvae, commonly called maggots. The larva has neither legs nor anything that can be recognized as a head. It does have a "mouth" and it can pull itself along by means of hooked bristles located at the mouth end. These bristles give off a fluid that helps to dissolve and digest the material on which the maggot is feeding. A fly maggot is really not much more than a mobile stomach and digestive system.

For five days or so the maggot feeds constantly and builds up fat until it splits its skin and molts. Molting is repeated several times. Finally, the larval feeding stops. Now the skin hardens into a rather tough and hard, brown pupal case. Here the maggot changes into an adult.

The adult fly has no jaws, and cannot chew its way out of the pupal case. It has a special organ for this purpose. Inside its head is a sack or pouch that can be pushed out through a crescent-shaped slit. Fluid is pumped into the sack, it pops out through the slit, and forces the end off the pupal case. Since pupation is likely to take place well down in the material the maggot fed on, it also uses this inflatable sack to force its way to the surface, pushing it out and pulling it in.

Eleven days is the average time from egg to adult. In the tropics or in temperate zone summers when the temperature is 80° F or above, it may take only a

20

week. If temperatures are low the process may take as long as a month. Because house flies can reproduce themselves with such remarkable speed, a number of naturalists and scientists have estimated how many offspring a male and female could be responsible for in a single season. One stated it in these terms: If two house flies mate in the spring and the female lays 120 eggs that all hatch, and all the resulting flies live and breed, within three months the descendants of the original pair would number about five and a half *quintillion*. This mass of flies would weigh billions of tons.

Where Do They Go in Winter?

An ever-intriguing question about house flies is: Where do they go in winter? There is no simple answer. House flies are very adaptable creatures, and what they do in one type of setting will not hold true in another. In temperate countries most adults die by autumn either from old age or disease. If there are fairly warm buildings in which they can hide away and find a bit of food, however, some may live through the winter. But most of the house flies that begin flying around soon after spring warmth begins emerge from larvae or pupae that were in a resting state over the winter. In extremely cold climates adults take refuge in such buildings as cow barns. Warmed by animal heat and supplied with food in the form of body wastes from the animals, the flies live and breed throughout the winter and into the spring.

Biting Flies and Blue Bottles

Upon occasion it seems that house flies start biting viciously, attacking anyone they can reach. This happens most often in rainy or damp weather. If flies bite, they are not true house flies. Quite likely they are stable flies (*Stomoxys calcitrans*) that breed in many places, but especially in stables. They are shorter than house flies and have a more rounded abdomen. They, too, like to come indoors, particularly just before a storm.

There is an important difference between stable flies and house flies. House flies have soft, sponge-like mouth parts that mop up their food—anything liquid or that they can liquefy with their saliva. But the stable fly has a thin, hard, pierc-

Stable fly—
Stomoxys calcitrans

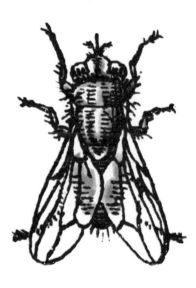

Blue bottle—
Calliphora vicina

Cluster fly—
Pollina rudis

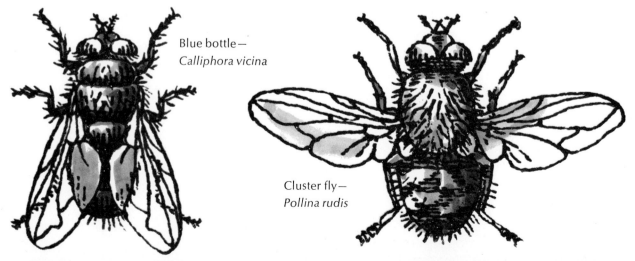

ing mouth part. Blood is the only food it seeks. And unlike some biting flies where only the female is bloodthirsty, both sexes are addicted. They regularly attack domestic and wild animals. But indoors, the ankles, arms, and necks of humans prove good feeding grounds.

Still another fly that goes indoors very readily is the blow fly, popularly known as the blue bottle. Blue bottles enter a house willingly but then seem quite frantic to get out again. They are attracted to light, and often meet their end under a fly swatter as they clamber over a window pane on a sunny day.

A female blue bottle does not lay eggs. Instead her eggs develop inside her body and hatch there so that she actually gives birth to living larvae. These she deposits in many places—often on meat, fish, or cheese if they happen to be exposed, particularly on rotten meat and on cuts and wounds of living animals. The larvae burrow into such food, eating as they burrow.

Because of their liking for decaying raw meat and festering cuts, blow flies often deposit their living larvae in cuts and natural openings of the body. Several species do this by preference and their larvae feed on living tissue. The larvae are often eaten accidentally. When this happens the hardy maggots continue to grow and, as a result of irritating the stomach and intestine, cause nausea, vomiting, and severe diarrhea.

All Gather Round

A housewife busy with fall cleaning is often startled to find not just one or two flies in her house, but groups of eight or ten. She may discover them behind pictures, among the books, or in other secluded spots.

Chances are, the insects have just made their way indoors. It is also likely that they are not ordinary house flies but are cluster flies (*Pollina rudis*). They look very much like house flies, but their wings overlap, giving them an elongated appearance. The popular name of this fly is based on its habit of gathering in clusters indoors, especially in the fall.

In late summer or early autumn when temperatures begin to drop as the sun goes down, cluster flies leave the fields and meadows, their usual habitat. By late afternoon they settle on roofs or upper walls that face south or southwest so that they receive warmth from the sun until it sets. Then they crawl into any tiny crack they can find. While the daytime temperatures remain in the range of 60° F to 70° F they creep outside again in the morning and back at night. But they soon are ready to settle down. If they can find a place in an attic or other hiding place where they will be undisturbed, they may spend the entire winter there.

A strange fact of the cluster fly's life story is that the larvae eat their way into the bodies of earthworms and develop there—one larva to a worm. The vast numbers of cluster flies are a reminder of how many earthworms there must be in the soil, often many thousands to an acre.

Tsetse fly —
Glossina palpalis

The Tsetse

It is difficult to believe that one small family of flies can affect the fate of a nation or continent. But this has happened and is still happening. The continent: Africa. The fly: the tsetse. These dangerous insects, looking rather like large, brightly colored house flies, are found only in tropical and subtropical Africa.

Tsetse flies carry and spread African sleeping sickness, a deadly disease. People who have the disease and do not die may become chronic invalids, unable to work or earn a living. Besides the damage they do to humans, tsetse flies spread related diseases that are fatal to cattle, horses, and wild animals.

23

SPREAD OF SLEEPING SICKNESS

African sleeping sickness is spread through equatorial Africa

Tsetse flies and sleeping sickness became known almost as soon as Europeans began to tap the riches of Africa. The first wealth to come from Africa was founded on slavery, the infamous trade in human begins. Slavers, who inspected their victims carefully to see whether they could stand the cruel voyage to the great West Indian slave markets, quickly learned that any captives with swollen lumps in their necks would soon sicken and die. Swollen neck glands are one of the early symptoms of sleeping sickness.

At that time no one suspected that fly bites had anything to do with the disease. It was the fifteenth century. The idea that these insects could cause a disease would not be accepted until a long way in the future. For almost three hundred years, until the late eighteenth century, most of Africa was unexplored. Europeans hugged the coasts, trading for whatever goods—slaves, mostly—that African tribesmen and Arab traders brought from the interior. In the eighteenth century things changed. Spurred by the desire to establish control over the gold trade and to claim land for their kings, the British and Portuguese began to invade the interior. Some of the first expeditions were nearly defeated by tsetse flies. Before the explorers reached their goals most of their horses and mules died of an unknown disease. Although the disease that killed their animals was new to the Portuguese and English fortune hunters, they soon recognized that flies were at the root of the trouble.

Little was known about these insects—how, for example, they differed from flies in the explorers' home countries, how they might be eliminated, or exactly what it was that caused the death of their animals. One hundred years later the situation had not changed very much. Late in the nineteenth century an Englishman wrote: "It is difficult to overestimate the importance of the part played by this noxious little insect [the tsetse] in preventing the opening up of Central Africa."

24

The tsetse fly family is a small one. Now found only in Africa, there is evidence that some tsetse flies lived on the North American continent in far-distant pre-historic times. There are only twenty-one different kinds, all belonging to a single genus, *Glossina*. Tsetse flies, like stable flies, have piercing mouth parts, and they feed on blood. Any kind of vertebrate blood is acceptable—mammal, bird, or reptile. They show no interest in dead animals, and they do not feed on open cuts or wounds. They specialize in fresh blood, and this is the reason they are so dangerous.

Sleeping sickness is called an infectious disease. Infectious diseases are caused by some living thing, plant or animal. When a person "catches" a disease, the germ that causes it has somehow gotten into his body from the outside. In order for infectious diseases to spread, three conditions are necessary: a source of germs, a carrier of the germs (called a *vector*), and a person or animal who is not immune to the germs.

Tsetse flies are the vectors of African sleeping sickness because they feed on blood. The germ of sleeping sickness is an animal, a microscopic one-celled animal called a *trypanosome*. When a tsetse fly takes its meal of blood from a person or animal that has the trypanosome in his blood, the tiny animals are swallowed right along with the blood. They enter the fly's digestive system and multiply there. Then they migrate through the fly's body and come to rest in its saliva glands.

Tsetse flies' saliva and that of all other bloodsucking flies, too, contains a chemical that keeps blood from clotting—keeps it flowing as long as the fly's beak is inserted under its victim's skin. The biting tsetse fly pumps its anti-clotting

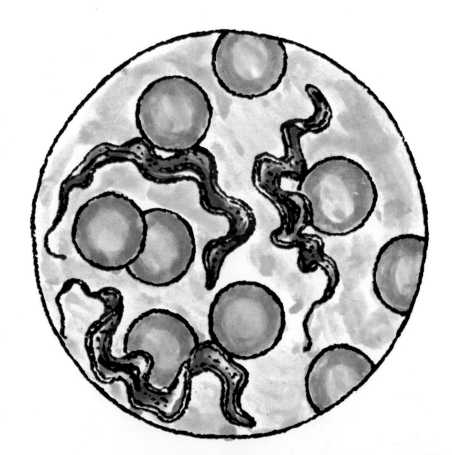

Trypanosome

saliva into its victim's blood and along with it go the trypanosomes. If the person—or animal—is *susceptible* (not immune) and if he gets a large enough injection of trypanosome, he will come down with the disease.

There are several kinds of trypanosomes and several kinds of tsetse flies. Not all of the flies carry all trypanosomes. Tsetse flies are divided into three groups. Two carry the trypanosomes that cause fatal illness to grazing animals. A third group contains several flies that transmit human sleeping sickness.

Early explorers did not seem to complain about infections attacking men—only animals. Apparently they were fortunate enough to escape being bitten by the "right kind" of fly. It seems likely, however, that many Africans were suffering greatly as a result of the tsetse flies.

There was a good reason why Europeans weren't often infected with sleeping sickness. Until the late nineteenth century human sleeping sickness was found mostly in only a small area of West Africa. Colonization changed this situation.

Among the benefits the English and other colonial powers brought to Africa was law and order and an end to the tribal warfare that had kept many tribes confined to their own territories. But tribal warfare had also kept the sources of trypanosomes localized. Under European-enforced peace of colonial days the tribesmen began to move about, to seek new grazing lands or places to live. Many Africans were also transported far from their own homes to work in mines and on ranches. Result: The sources of human trypanosomes spread from West Africa straight across to the Indian Ocean. Sleeping sickness now exists in the Congo region, Uganda, Kenya, Tanzania, Zambia, and Rhodesia.

At the beginning of the twentieth century human sleeping sickness was given serious study for the first time when a serious epidemic broke out in a wide area north of Lake Victoria. The epidemic lasted for eight years, killing thousands, and continued to rage until most of the survivors were evacuated from the region.

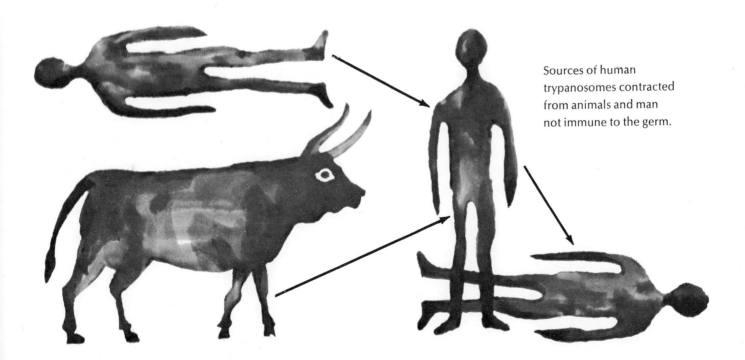

Sources of human trypanosomes contracted from animals and man not immune to the germ.

Nagana, the animal form of sleeping sickness, is also widespread in the tropical African highlands. More than two million square miles are closed to cattle raising. In a land where protein is short, this is a great tragedy, for many people in the region suffer from malnutrition. The fly that hindered African exploration now continues to hinder the development of its new nations. Because of the great harm they do, to both man and animals, tsetse flies have been given a tremendous amount of attention by scientists.

The relationship between the source of germs, the vector or carrier, and the susceptible person is known as the "chain of infection." Control of a disease calls for breaking the chain. For example, polio has been controlled by mass immunization, breaking the chain by making the person immune. But attempts to control sleeping sickness and nagana have been centered on eliminating the tsetse fly itself.

The tsetse fly has never been brought completely under control. One reason is because the various species do not lay eggs. The eggs remain in the female's body and develop into larvae fed by special glands. When the larva is full grown and ready to pupate, it is dropped to the ground where it instantly burrows into the soil. There it passes into its pupal stage. In thirty days the adult is ready to emerge and begin searching for blood. The eggs develop one at a time, and there is no set number that a single fly may produce. Control would be much easier if the eggs and larvae developed in the open or in large masses, as is the case with malaria-carrying mosquitoes.

Attempts to destroy tsetse flies have included stripping large areas of their vegetation. Tsetse flies rest in shade and will quickly disperse if it is not present. When the flies are spread out over a wide area they do not breed so frequently. Another method has been to make specially designed traps in which large numbers could be caught. Even such drastic measures as killing all antelopes and other wild animals that might be harboring the trypanosomes have been considered but not carried out. Today the tsetses are better confined than formerly, and new areas are being opened up for cattle ranching.

For years the World Health Organization and other United Nations agencies have been pushing for programs that would eliminate the tsetse for all time. Progress was made, and in 1960 there were only two thousands known cases of sleeping sickness in the Congo. In 1966 there were about ten thousand. The increase was due to the chaos that followed moves for national independence, and to a lack of doctors and trained workers.

But efforts will continue. The economic development of the African continent depends in part on vanquishing the trouble-making tsetse.

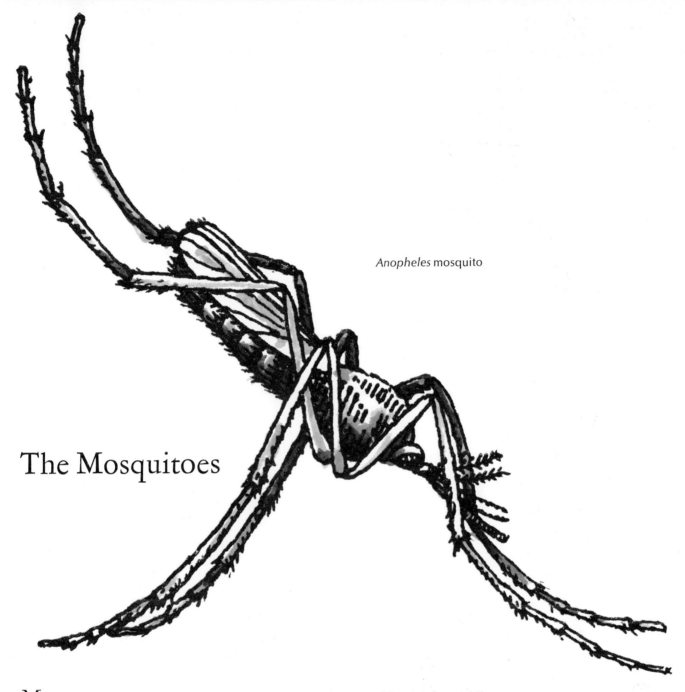

Anopheles mosquito

The Mosquitoes

Mosquitoes, like their distant relatives the tsetse flies, are bloodsuckers. All man's problems with mosquitoes arise from the fact that, for their eggs to develop, the female must have at least one meal of blood. Thus they bite, and their bites leave annoying, itching lumps. Almost as bad as their bites is the high-pitched, sleep-shattering whine of female mosquitoes on the hunt.

Mosquito bites alone are reason enough for constant war on these pesky insects. Great swarms of them have delayed agricultural or industrial developments until the swamps and bogs where they were breeding were drained. Areas that would otherwise make ideal vacation spots have been abandoned or left underdeveloped just because of the mosquitoes' itching bites, but all these losses are slight when compared to the damage done to man and his animals by mosquito-borne diseases.

29

Common *Culex* mosquito

In certain areas of the world mosquitoes are the most dreaded of all creatures. Malaria—a disease spread only by certain mosquitoes—has brought suffering and death to millions, and still does. Yellow fever, for centuries a great menace in tropical regions, flourished because of certain species of mosquitoes. Mostly we think of mosquitoes and the diseases they carry as problems of underdeveloped tropical areas, but this is an error. Malaria was quite common in the United States until the early years of the present century. Two serious and sometimes deadly diseases, known as St. Louis sleeping sickness and equine (horse) encephalitis, still occur in the United States. Almost every year there are outbreaks of these diseases transmitted by the common house mosquito.

Control measures against mosquitoes are aimed at the larvae or the adults. Eradication may involve drainage of the larval habitats, or treatment of the larval habitat.

Members of the family *Culicidae*, the mosquito family, are found almost every place on earth, from regions close to the Arctic circle to the most remote desert oases. Wherever man lives so do mosquitoes. To the question how many kinds of mosquitoes are there, the only answer is an educated guess. Two thousand species is a number commonly given, but no one knows for sure.

Each species has its preferences in dwelling places, breeding spots, flying time, and favorite kind of blood. Some thrive in tropical weather, others do best in the temperate regions. A few are adapted to the long, cool summer days of the near Arctic areas. There are day fliers, night fliers, dusk and dawn fliers. Several species seek the blood of birds and chickens, some bite reptiles and frogs, and the common house mosquito seems to prefer human blood. A few—a very few—do not seem to feed on blood at all. Instead they feed on plant juices and the nectar of blossoms.

In studying insects one soon gets used to the fact that there are few hard and fast rules. For every general statement about insects there are many fascinating exceptions. Take, for example, one group of mosquitoes that drinks neither blood nor nectar, but gets its food from the mouths of ants. The hungry mosquito lands in front of a particular kind of ant, grasps it between her legs, and thrusts her beak into the ant's open jaws to drink the digested plant juices on which the ant has previously fed.

Still, in spite of the exceptions, almost all mosquitoes bite, and it is quite certain that most species require at least one meal of blood before the female can develop eggs that can produce living young.

Only females bite. Blood, it is thought, supplies protein, but this is by no means certain. Nor is it sure just what part of the blood is needed. Scientists have separated blood into cells and liquid (plasma) and fed mosquitoes on each. They could find no difference in egg-laying capacity.

A few female mosquitoes seem to be able to lay eggs without first helping themselves to a meal of human or animal blood. These females, like all male mos-

Gambusia eating mosquito larvae and eggs.

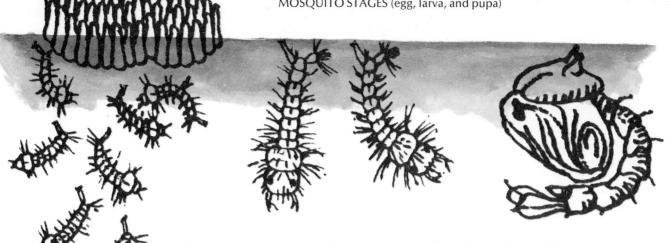

quitoes, apparently live on flower nectar or plant juices. One of those that can manage without blood is the common American house mosquito, *Culex pipiens*. Unfortunately, this does not keep the female from going after it. Mosquito eggs hatch in water and the larvae develop and pupate in water. Any kind of water may contain larvae. Wherever water stands, fresh or salt, clean or foul, a great amount or very little of it, there is at least one kind of mosquito that will lay eggs in it.

Mosquitoes breed in rain puddles, ponds, and creeks. Old tire casings and tin cans also provide breeding places. Quite a few mosquitoes breed in the water found in tree holes and old stumps, and one species lays its eggs only in the water caught in the leaves of pitcher plants. Its larvae feed on bits of decaying insects trapped by the insect-catching plants. But of all breeding places for mosquitoes, swamps, bogs, and marshes are the most important.

The reason that so much attention is given to where mosquitoes breed is that the best way to control mosquito-borne diseases is by wiping out the mosquitoes. This is done most easily by killing the larvae, or by draining the water in which they develop.

Some mosquitoes lay eggs in moving water, but a close look will reveal that the eggs are actually deposited in a sheltered place—under stones or plants, or in quiet spots so that the currents will not wash away the eggs or larvae. A few species lay eggs on the ground, but always in moist areas. These eggs can begin to develop only after rain has covered them or washed them into a pool or puddle.

House mosquitoes prefer artificial containers for their eggs and are often called rain-barrel mosquitoes. Tin cans, garbage cans, or any container of water will do quite nicely for the female. She sits on the surface and lays her eggs one at a time. Each egg is carefully placed against another until a tiny raft of two or three dozen is formed, all glued together with a sticky substance she produces along with her eggs.

The malaria-spreading mosquitoes of the genus *Anopheles* lay their eggs in quite a different way. The female doesn't sit on the water but carries on a lively dance several inches above the surface, dropping her eggs as she bobs up and down.

32

MALARIA CYCLE

1 Sporozoite stage of the Plasmodium introduced into blood stream with mosquito saliva.

2 Trophozoite stage in which the Plasmodium feeds on the red blood cell.

Mosquito-egg rafts are the favorite food of many minnows who feed at the surface and are called, reasonably enough, top minnows.

Two families of top minnows are such important mosquito killers that they have been transported practically all over the world for this purpose. Their names are the mosquito fish (*Gambusia*) and killifish. *Gambusia* has been stocked extensively in the irrigation streams in California and in Texas and other southwestern states. Mosquito eggs, like the eggs of all flies, hatch into larvae that bear no resemblance to the adults they will become. There are countless variations in the way mosquito larvae behave. Most often, however, the wigglers, as they are called, feed by vibrating tiny brush- or comb-like parts. This causes a current of water to flow toward the wiggler's mouth and from this it strains out the tiny bits of food it lives on. Not all wigglers are so peaceful. Some attack and eat other wigglers just about as big as themselves. Still others gnaw on submerged plant stems or scrape off the stems small insects or other water life.

Although mosquito larvae are water animals, most come to the surface to breathe. Some bob up and down, making regular trips to the surface for air. Others stay just under the surface and breathe through a little tube or siphon located in their tails. When disturbed by either a shadow or a strong ripple, the larvae drop quickly from the surface and stay quietly submerged for ten minutes or more.

While surface breathing is the general rule, not all mosquitoes do it. Some, including the dangerous *Anopheles* mosquitoes, are gill breathers or take dissolved oxygen from water through their skins. Three groups get their oxygen either from the surface of submerged plant leaves or directly from the plant tissues

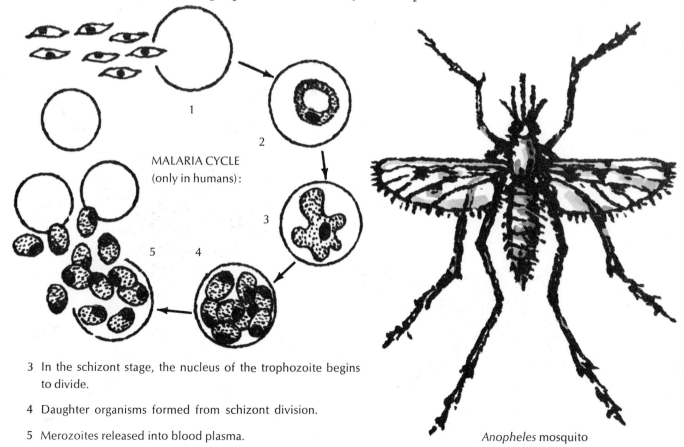

MALARIA CYCLE
(only in humans):

3 In the schizont stage, the nucleus of the trophozoite begins to divide.

4 Daughter organisms formed from schizont division.

5 Merozoites released into blood plasma.

Anopheles mosquito

by means of siphons equipped with little saw-like structures that can pierce stems or roots.

Without any known exception all mosquito larvae shed their skins exactly four times. The time this takes differs from species to species. Within a species the time required for an egg to hatch, go through its four larval stages, pupate and emerge as an adult, also varies. Temperature is the most important thing in the process—the warmer the faster, up to a point. When the water temperature gets over 80° F, however, growth is either slowed down or the larva dies.

Compared with most insects, mosquitoes go from egg to adult in fairly short order. Pupation is short, too, ranging from twenty-four hours to two or three days.

Where mosquito eggs are laid in small puddles that dry up quickly, the whole process—egg to adult—must take place quickly. Those species that breed in permanently wet places may take longer.

Egg, larva, pupa, adult, all in a few days. That is the way the mosquito's life cycle usually goes. Sometimes when conditions are not favorable for this age-old rhythm, a remarkable change of schedule may take place. Growth and development stop suddenly. Life goes on but no changes take place until conditions are again favorable. This built-in delaying action is known as *diapause*. It occurs in almost all insects and at various stages. Among mosquitoes diapause occurs almost always in the egg stage, and probably makes survival possible from one year to the next.

For example, many of the mosquitoes that live in the cold climates of both hemispheres lay their eggs all summer long. The late summer eggs—or some of them—do not hatch but go into diapause and lie inactive into fall and through the winter. The next spring the eggs hatch, even after being frozen for months at subzero temperatures. Egg diapause also occurs among those mosquitoes that breed where the water is likely to dry up fast.

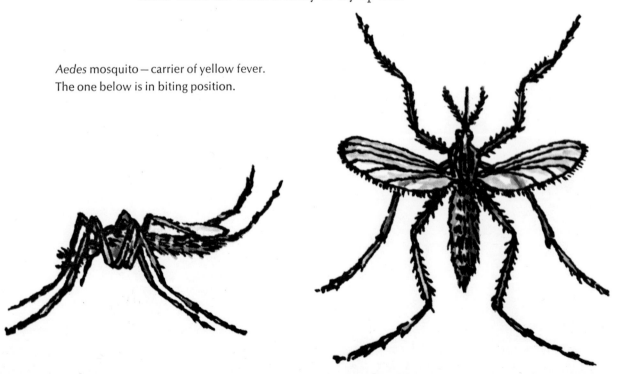

Aedes mosquito—carrier of yellow fever.
The one below is in biting position.

Like all things in insect study there are no hard and fast rules about diapause, and while diapause has been carefully observed and described it is not very well understood. Some tropical mosquitoes, for instance, regularly go through egg diapause even though there is no apparent reason—at least that scientists can see. Nor do scientists understand just what it is that triggers diapause to begin and end. Clearly if it began just when the unfavorable conditions took place, it would be too late. If diapause of over-wintering eggs ended at a warm spell or midwinter thaw it would do no good either. The one thing that seems most likely to control the beginning and end of the inactive period is daylight. This would ensure against too early an end of diapause as the result of midwinter thaws.

Mosquitoes, Yellow Fever, and Malaria U. S. 1528755

A hundred years ago everyone considered mosquitoes a terrible nuisance just as we do today, but nothing more. No scientist or physician believed, or even seriously considered, that there was any connection between mosquito bites and disease. In fact the few daring souls who had suggested such an idea were considered either fools or madmen by their scientific friends.

In the late 1880's the French businessmen who had successfully built the Suez Canal started to dig through the swamps and jungles of the Isthumus of Panama to make a waterway from Atlantic to Pacific. They had no idea that the swarms of viciously biting mosquitos were more than a devilish nuisance. Digging began in 1879 and came to an unsuccessful end in 1889, after tens of thousands of workers had died from malaria and yellow fever. The financiers of Europe and their engineers had been defeated by two mosquitoes, the *Aedes* mosquito, which transmits yellow fever, and the *Anopheles* mosquito, the carrier of malaria.

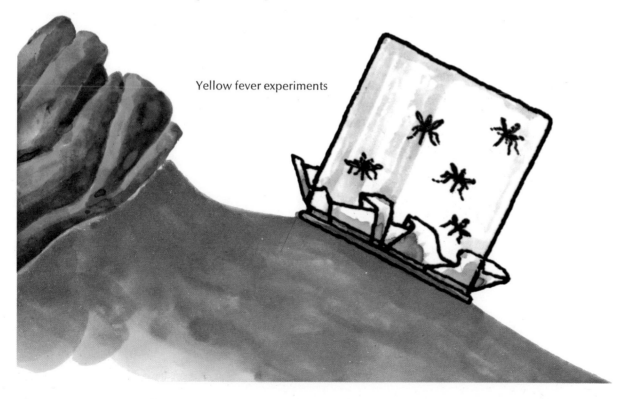

Yellow fever experiments

Fifteen years later the United States, recognizing the importance of a canal to its military and commercial interests, took over from France. President Theodore Roosevelt appointed William Crawford Gorgas as chief of disease-control efforts. The battle against mosquitoes was begun. By 1906 yellow fever was under control. Malaria and the *Anopheles* mosquitoes proved tougher enemies. It was 1913 before it could be claimed that the Canal Zone was relatively free of malaria.

In the few years between the French defeat and the American victory, important discoveries had been made. Actually the story began in 1884 when Patrick Manson, a Scottish physician working in China, proved that the *filaria,* a kind of worm that makes humans ill, is carried by mosquitoes. Manson was later knighted by his queen for this discovery.

Another Scot, Ronald Ross, a doctor working for the East India Company, picked up Manson's work and applied it to malaria. By 1900, Ross and others had worked out how malaria is carried by the mosquitoes with dappled wings—the *Anopheles.* They also found the tiny one-celled animal that actually causes the disease and traced its life cycle in mosquito and man, where it lives in human blood.

While Manson, Ross, and others were working on malaria, four Americans—Walter Reed, James Carroll, Aristides Agrammonti, and Jesse Lazear—were proving in the most dramatic possible way that mosquitoes were responsible for yellow fever. The Americans were working in Cuba trying to do something—anything—to control the raging yellow fever that was killing hundreds of American soldiers stationed there following the Spanish American War.

The American doctors had heard from Carlos Finlay, a physician in Havana, that a mosquito transmitted yellow fever. In Havana, Finlay was thought to be a little less than completely sane, but Reed and his co-workers had tried everything with no success. They were ready to try any idea at all, even if its proponent was considered odd.

From eggs they raised *Aedes aegypti* mosquitoes, the kind Finlay said carried the disease. The adults were fed on patients ill with yellow fever. Then, to complete the experiment, the valiant scientists took a desperate but necessary chance. They let the mosquitoes feed on their own bare arms. A few days later James Carroll came down with the disease and nearly died. Jesse Lazear was not so lucky. Five days after he fed mosquitoes on his arm he was racked with fever. On the sixth day he died.

Gorgas, armed with the discoveries of Manson, Ross, Reed, and the others, knew what the enemy was and organized the greatest and most successful anti-insect campaign ever seen. He attacked mosquitoes in every possible way. Pools and ditches were drained or filled. Large areas were sprayed with oil so that larvae couldn't breathe. He cleaned underbrush where the adults rested, screened sleeping quarters and mess tents. In 1914 the Panama Canal was opened.

A Menace to Mammals

Fly bites can drive animals almost crazy with pain and sometimes cause their death. In almost any way that can be imagined for an insect to annoy an animal there is at least one—often more—species of flies that does it. There are blood-sucking flies, flies that lay their eggs in cuts and sores, flies whose larvae eat the living flesh of animals. Besides all the damage they do directly, flies transmit serious and deadly diseases among animals.

The family *Tabanidae* is particularly known for its vicious and voracious biting habits. The big, noisy horse flies, and the persistent, painfully biting deer flies are tabanids. Their prime targets are livestock and wild animals, but in the absence of their usual source of blood, they turn their unwelcome attention to humans. Just as bad are flies belonging to the family *Simuliidae*, the black flies and punkies.

Black flies are well known to anyone who has ever spent any time in either

Black horse fly — *Tabanus atratus*

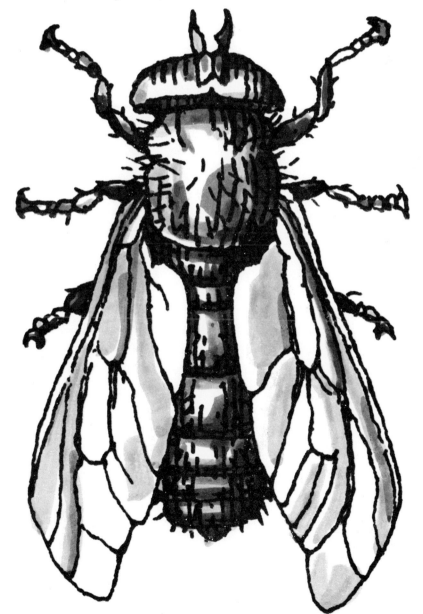

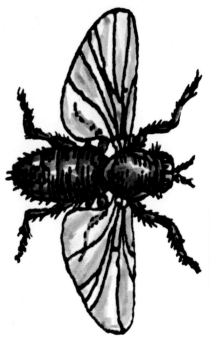

Black fly—
Simulium species

Black fly larva

Black fly pupa

northern woodlands or tropical forests. Only the females bite, and they attack any bit of exposed skin and leave an intensely itching blood blister. So persistent and aggressive is their pursuit of human beings that victims of black fly bites are surprised to find that humans are not their main source of blood. Actually any warm-blooded animal will do. Black fly bites are not only painful, but mildly poisonous. They have been known to cause severe sickness.

A report from Yugoslavia indicates just how much damage black flies can do. Nearly twenty thousand animals—horses, cows, sheep, and goats—were killed in a single year when black flies were at their peak of activity. Made nervous by repeated fly bites, the helpless animals stopped grazing and finally died from the combined efforts of starvation and loss of blood.

The typical black fly is fat, short-legged, and humpbacked. Many species really are black, but others are brightly tinted with yellow, orange, and red. There is even a white-stockinged black fly.

Swift-flowing streams are the homes of black fly larvae. Each larva attaches itself to a rock by spinning a silken thread to which it holds with a special sucker as it feeds on tiny bits of food brought along by the rushing water. Masses of the larvae sometimes look like large black patches on the stream bottom.

The fully grown black fly larva spins itself a cocoon of silk. Just before it begins to pupate, the downstream end of the cocoon is pushed open. The pupa breathes the air dissolved in the water and filters it into the space just under its silken case. Soon the air-bloated cocoon looks like a tiny balloon. It pops to the surface and a fully grown black fly emerges from the opening.

Misery for Horses and Deer

One thing can be said in favor of the horse fly: It does not sneak up on its victims. Instead it comes roaring in with a loud whirr-r-r-r. Some horse flies, as anyone knows who has ever been bitten, are very large, almost an inch in length. Others are of medium size, not much larger than a house fly. All are broad and heavy in build. Their bites usually hurt enough to call forth a loud "ouch," and make a small but definite blood-oozing hole.

In pastures and open country where there are numbers of horses, cattle, and other domestic animals, horse flies often exist in abundance. Where they do, any animal in the pastures is likely to have open sores on its neck, back, and legs. These sores develop because the flies bite once, and then return again and again to the same spot, which soon begins to fester. Sometimes the big animals run frantically around paddocks or pastures in a hopeless effort to avoid their tormentors.

One particularly aggressive horse fly is well known to picnickers and bathers along the Atlantic coast. This is the one whose painful bite can cause a beach party to pack up and leave. Besides producing sores, the flies may transmit diseases to horses, cattle, or sheep. Man, too, may become infected by the germs they carry.

Cleg—
Haematopota pluvalis

Deer flies belong to the same family as the horse flies. Popularly they are called a variety of names including gad flies, clegs, and ear flies. Less polite names are also used by those who are bitten. These pests live in woodlands where their natural prey are wild animals, ranging in size from rabbits to deer. Any human who gets within range is fair game, however. Some species seem to concentrate on hands and wrists; others specialize on necks and heads.

Although their attack is just as painful, the largest deer fly is about the size of the smallest horse fly. Unlike their large relative, deer flies are a silent menace. No buzzing or humming warns the victim of the sharp, stabbing bite to come. The bites are not only painful, but also potentially dangerous, because these insects transmit diseases to both humans and animals. One case is reported where deer flies caused the closing of a camp after thirty young men contracted tularemia or rabbit fever from their bites. Here again, the females do the biting. Males feed on flowers.

The misery brought about by horse flies and deer flies is almost unbelievable. In ancient times they plagued herdsmen and their flocks and herds until the health of all was threatened. Even today a number of pastoral tribes in east Africa have no permanent home, but migrate each year in an attempt to get their cattle and camels away from the dreaded flies.

Bots and Warbles

Bot flies, warbles, and blow flies have habits to match their unattractive names. They are parasites and spend some part of their life cycle either on animals or inside them.

Deer fly—
Chrysops species

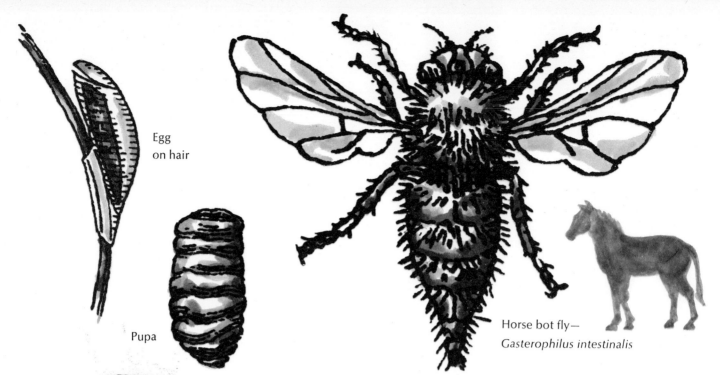

Egg
on hair

Pupa

Larva

Horse bot fly—
Gasterophilus intestinalis

Bot flies are rather large hairy creatures that look something like bees. They are described by their family name, *Gasterophilidae,* which, freely translated, means stomach lovers. All bot fly larvae spend most of their lives inside animals. The horse bot fly is a good example. Its larvae cling to the stomach lining and gorge on blood and predigested food.

The bot fly life cycle begins when the female darts in to lay her eggs on the hair of mules, donkeys, or horses. Each egg—they are laid one at a time—hatches into a rather thin, rough-skinned or spiny larva that tickles or itches the host animal. If the animal manages to reach the itchy spot and lick it, the newly hatched larva burrows into the skin of the tongue. In later stages it travels down the throat and goes into the stomach, where, with tiny hooks, it attaches itself to the stomach lining. There it spends the entire winter, feeding and growing while the infested animal suffers greatly.

In spring the fat larva—reddened with engorged blood—lets go its hold on the host and passes out with the animal's droppings. As soon as it reaches the ground, it becomes a pupa. By summer it is an adult, ready to mate and lay eggs.

Sheep bot flies are especially harmful parasites. The female deposits eggs, or sometimes larvae, in the nostrils of sheep or goats. During the winter and spring the larvae live in the nostrils or crawl into the sinuses, where they grow to more than an inch in length. If numerous, they can cause great pain and even death. The infected animal sometimes loses its balance and wobbles around as if drunk. When this happens the poor beast is said to have the blind staggers. Other flies closely related to the sheep bot thrive at the expense of a variety of mammals including rabbits, elephants, kangaroos, and humans.

Dermatobia hominis, a South American insect, is best known as the human bot fly, although its primary host is cattle. The larvae develop just under the skin of

40

either humans or cattle. Being air breathers, they maintain a hole through which they can breathe. Young larvae stay close to the surface, older larvae "dig in" as much as an inch and come up for air only occasionally. The feeling as they creep around is described as "quite unbelievable."

If the way human bot flies get their larvae to a suitable host had not been carefully observed many times, it, too, would be called unbelievable.

The female dermatobia doesn't lay eggs directly on the host's skin. Instead of hunting for a warm-blooded host, she seeks swampy areas where mosquitoes are emerging. She overtakes a mosquito, grasps it, and quickly attaches from ten to fifty tiny eggs to the underside of the mosquito's abdomen. Since the bot fly can't distinguish male mosquitoes from females, a good many eggs are fortunately wasted. Some of the egg-laden mosquitoes eventually land on a human or other warm-blooded animal and start to siphon off their necessary meal of blood. Heated both by the host's skin and its blood inside the mosquito, the bot fly eggs hatch while the mosquito is sucking blood. The tiny larvae burrow into the skin of their host and start feeding. To get out again when they are full grown, the larvae make the breathing holes larger and fall to the ground.

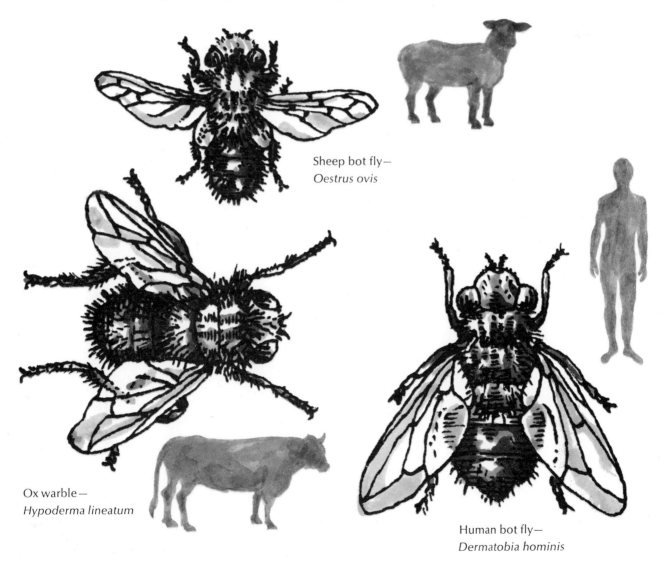

Sheep bot fly—
Oestrus ovis

Ox warble—
Hypoderma lineatum

Human bot fly—
Dermatobia hominis

Scientists are interested in bot flies because of their destructiveness and also because they are insect speed demons, or reported to be. One scientist who did his calculations on the basis of observing wing beats rather than the insect in motion reported that deer bot flies reach a top speed of 815 miles an hour. This story of a supersonic fly created quite a stir among entomologists as well as a great deal of careful study. Many studies of the question "How speedy is a bot fly?" have been made since. The answer turns out to be somewhat disappointing—about thirty to forty miles an hour. For short, darting flights the flies may go up to fifty miles an hour. Though this is far from their reputed speed, it is still impressive for a small creature to achieve under its own power.

Warbles

The family name of warble flies, *Hypodermidae,* coming from the same root as "hypodermic," should not require any explanation. The larvae of these flies dig their way under their host's skin, and when fully grown come back to rest under the skin of its back. Between times they wander around inside the host animal in the spaces between the internal organs and the muscles.

Warble is the name given to the tumor-like swelling that the fully grown larva makes on its host's back. After spending the winter there, the larva, now about an inch long, eats its way through the hide and falls to the ground to pupate. The holes ruin the hide for leather. Even worse, the meat near the warble—the meat that makes the best steaks—is ruined.

LIFE CYCLE OF THE WARBLE — *Hypoderma* species

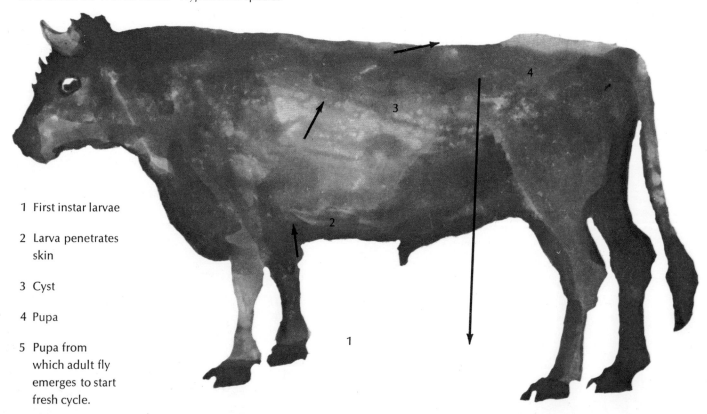

1 First instar larvae

2 Larva penetrates skin

3 Cyst

4 Pupa

5 Pupa from which adult fly emerges to start fresh cycle.

Tachinid—*Tachinidae*
on caterpillar

The Helpful Flies

After spending so much time with flies that are public enemies, it may be a pleasure to turn to some that are helpful. High on any list of helpful insects are the members of the family *Tachinidae*, commonly called the tachina flies or tachinids.

Tachina flies are hunters and killers, but their "victims" are neither humans nor domestic animals. Instead they feed on insects that attack food crops, especially the caterpillars of harmful moths. Beetles, grasshoppers, wasps, and other flies are also included on the tachina menu.

Tachinid flies—there are several species—usually lay their eggs right on the caterpillars they parasitize. A few female tachinids are equipped with a kind of boring extension on their abdomens. This they use to drill holes in caterpillars and to lay their eggs inside. Eggs are also laid on the grass or leaves where they will be swallowed by a foraging caterpillar, or sprayed from the air. While most of these flies are egg layers, the family also includes live bearers that deposit larvae either on the host insect or in some place where the host is likely to crawl.

In any case the tachinid larvae eat their way into the inside of the host and feed on its juices and living tissue. As the larvae grow, the host shrivels up and finally dies. Maturity of the larvae and death of the host caterpillars happen at the same time. The tachinid pupa rests in its victim's shriveled remains until the adult fly emerges.

43

Robber fly — *Asilidae*

Assassin fly—
Asilus Crabroniformis

An adult tachina is likely to be a fierce-looking, bristle-covered insect. Their habits don't match their appearance. In contrast to their carnivorous larvae, the adults drink nectar from flowers. Thus tachinids do double duty: The adults cross-pollinate flowers; the larvae destroy harmful insects.

A robber fly sounds like trouble. Robber flies, like tachinids, do not direct their activities against humans, however. The family is large; more than four thousand species live throughout the world. They vary in size but are inclined to be big. Some are almost two inches in length. Their color may be black, brown, or reddish. As larvae they feed on insects and probably on any soft-bodied creature to be found in rotting wood and leaves. As adults they boldly assault honeybees, wasps, and small bumble bees—all of which are caught on the wing.

The assassin fly is an especially swift robber fly of open, sunny fields. It overtakes its prey in midair, clutches the other insect in its legs, and with a sharp jab of its beak squirts in a drop of its saliva, which acts as an anesthetic. The assassin then carries its victim's limp body to a convenient spot and dines on its body fluid.

Aids to Science

If the house fly is the world's best-known fly, second honors must go to *Drosophila melanogaster*. Not many people recognize this name, but nearly everyone who speaks English is familiar with "fruit fly" or "vinegar fly"—two of the popular names commonly used for the small insect with the long scientific name. One reason fruit flies are so well known is that they are so widespread; they live successfully indoors or out, in cities and in the country all over the world. But the most important reason for their fame is their use in experimental studies in genetics and heredity.

Although all fruit flies look pretty much the same to us, they do, just like humans, vary quite a bit among themselves. There are races and strains of *Drosophila* that have quite definite characteristics. Red is the color of most *Drosophila* eyes, but there are also white-eyed fruit flies and some with a red eye crossed with a white bar. The wings vary too. Some flies have shriveled, club-like wings.

Scientists found that, when a red-eyed fly is mated with a white-eyed fly, the offspring are red-eyed. When two red-eyed flies of this generation are mated, however, something quite unexpected happens. Some offspring are red-eyed, some white-eyed. And it was discovered that white-eyed flies never produce red-eyed flies. By breeding tens of thousands of flies in hundreds of generations and keeping careful records of how such characteristics as eye color and wing shape are passed on from parents to offspring, the geneticists hit upon an important idea.

They knew that when the flies mate, sperm cells from male flies joined with egg cells of females. Thus, they reasoned, each egg and each sperm gives half the material to the flies that will result from the mating. They also reasoned that something in the eggs and sperms carried the characteristics from parents to young. When the young flies mature and produce egg cells and sperm cells, however, these materials are sorted out again by definite rules and passed on. Thus the scientists could explain why a white-eyed fly and a red-eyed fly had red-eyed offspring, but could have grandchildren with eyes of each color. The scientists also discovered another thing: The cell material that controls eye color is quite separate from the material that controls wing shape and other characteristics. "Gene" was the name given to each bit of character-controlling material. There were, according to the scientists, eye-color genes and wing-shape genes. In fact there is at last one gene for every characteristic of every living thing.

From what they knew about the material inside egg and sperm cells, the sci-

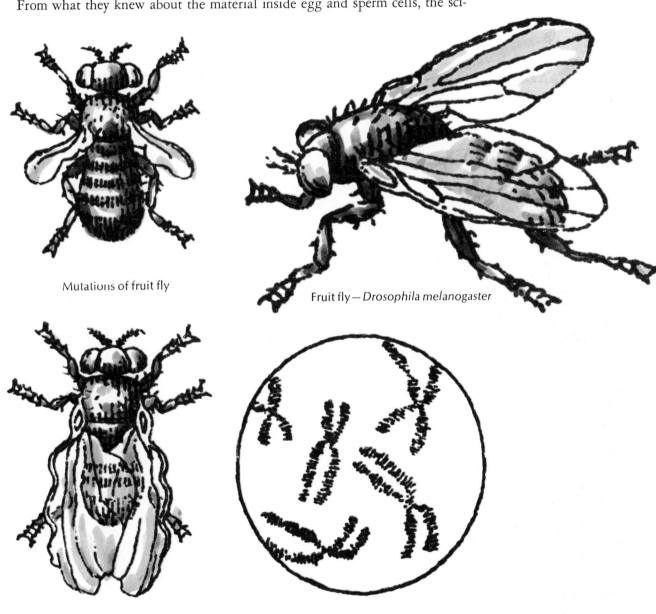

Mutations of fruit fly

Fruit fly — *Drosophila melanogaster*

Chromosomes of the fruit fly

Syrphid—*Syrphidae*

Merodon equestris

Narcissus bulb damage by larva of Syrphid fly

entists had a pretty good idea of where these genes were located. Up to this point no one had ever seen a gene; they were simply a "made-up" explanation that seemed to work. "This," said the scientists, "is a reasonable idea and we can use it to predict ahead of time the results that experiments will show." Most of this idea was worked out from fruit fly experiments by an American, Thomas Hunt Morgan. Morgan was given a Nobel Prize for his work.

The usefulness of the fruit fly was not over. The tiny insect had two more gifts for science.

Looking at a fruit fly—they are not quite one quarter inch long—it's hard to believe they have any part that could be called large. They do however have unusually large *chromosomes* in their saliva glands. Chromosomes are rather wormlike structures found in the center of cells. All cells have them. The gene idea made it quite clear that (1) if there really are genes (2) they must be located on the chromosomes. Sure enough: It turned out that the giant chromosomes in the fruit fly's saliva glands could be mapped; certain parts of the chromosomes were shown to carry the material that controlled specific characteristics.

Genes are not likely to change. If they were, then it would have been impossible to work out the ideas scientists developed to explain why young creatures resemble their parents. Yet, careful watching of generation after generation demonstrated that sometimes a new characteristic appeared. Some genes must change. *Mutation* is the name given to a changed gene.

Herman Mueller, an American scientist, made a long and careful study of mutations. Then he showed he could produce such changes—create mutations—by X-raying fruit flies. Mueller became the second American to win a Nobel Prize for his work in genetics.

Another family of helpful flies—the syrphids—has members that are a remarkable aid to farmers. These insects are known as flower flies or hover flies. You may see them in groups of a dozen or more on a sunny day along country lanes or woodland paths, hovering some eight or ten feet above the flowers. As they feed, they carry pollen from blossom to blossom.

Syrphids not only pollinate flowers; in the larval stage they feed on plant lice (aphids), on mealy bugs, and other insects that desroy plants. Creeping around by means of mouth hooks, the larvae attack agricultural pests and suck out their vital juices.

A North African hover fly (*India fasciata*) preys on the eggs of locusts. The little female fly reaches the hidden locust eggs by burrowing several inches into hard soil. Generations of these flies can be of help in reducing the scope of locust plagues. Not all the digging hover flies are welcome in gardens. Some produce larvae that dig into bulbs for their nourishment. One species concentrates on narcissus bulbs, another attacks the bulbs of ornamental flowers and root crops such as onions.

Mydas clavatus

Big and Little

Crane flies, the largest of all Diptera, look like super mosquitoes. Fortunately they have no biting or piercing equipment and are harmless. Their food needs are simple; they require only a little sugar from the nectar of flowers, and water. Many feed on vegetation growing in swampy areas.

In the more than six thousand species in this family (*Tipulidae*) there are naturally a number of variations in appearance. In general, they may be recognized by these features: long, slender wings and bodies, and especially long legs. The dangerous looking, spear-like projection at the rear of a female's body is not a stinger, but an ovipositor with which she lays her eggs in the ground.

Some tropical crane flies have a wingspread of almost four inches. Big ones are found in temperate climates, too. Several species common in the United States have legs long enough, when outspread, to cover a small saucer. Size, however, is almost never an important characteristic in classifying insects. Family groups are set up on characteristics such as mouth parts, antennae shape, the location of the joints between segments. So it is not unusual to find that crane fly sizes vary with species all the way down to the one that is a mere sixth of an inch long, the "snow fly" of the northern United States and Canada. It is one of a few species whose wings have dwindled to nothing, or almost nothing.

"Normal" crane flies, big though their wings are, do not excel as fliers. They fly clumsily, with the second and third pairs of legs dragging behind and the first pair doubled up in front. Because of their slow flight, crane flies are easily preyed on by birds and by swift and predatory flies.

47

Crane fly larvae are found, depending on the species, in decaying wood or in moss. The larvae of one species are frequently called "leather-jackets" because the round, grub-like body is protected by a tough covering. Leather-jackets feed on roots of all kinds, including grass. Often they cause a once-attractive lawn to look like a disaster area. The pupae work up to the surface of the soil with stiff bristles and leave their empty cases sticking up in close-cropped lawns. Crane flies are not the only giant Diptera. The family *Mydaidae* that is closely related to the robber flies has its share of big ones, too. *Mydas heros*, a handsome red and black native of South America, is two inches long. Its wings spread out three inches. Several of the family live on the North American continent. *Mydas luteipennis*, with large orange wings, is found in the southwestern states and in Mexico. *Mydas clavatus*, with a wingspread of about two inches, is velvety, black-banded, with bright orange-red on the abdomen. It is found in northern and eastern states.

Tiny but Terrible

At the other end of the size scale are most members of the midge family. There are two kinds—land midges and water midges. Those that develop in water are food for fish. They hatch in incredible numbers. The fisherman fails

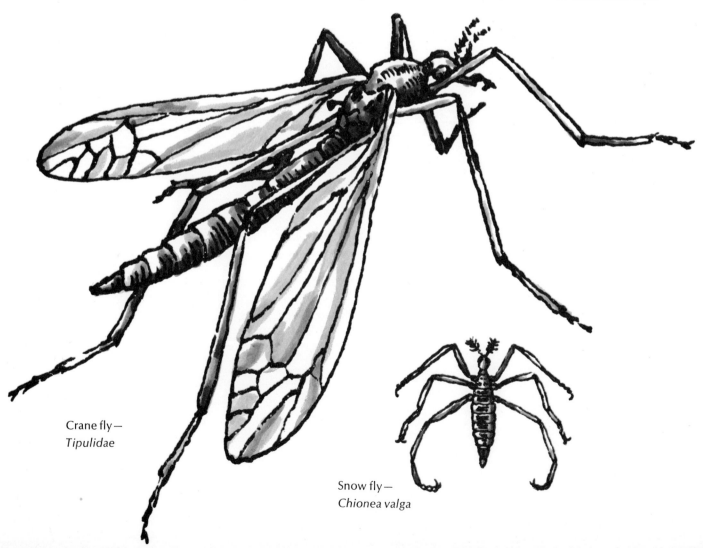

Crane fly—
Tipulidae

Snow fly—
Chionea valga

to appreciate the adult midges, however. Though most kinds cannot bite, they swarm about his head, crawl into his eyes, ears, nose, and even mouth.

One kind of midge that *can* bite is popularly known by several different names including sand flies, punkies, and no-see-ums. They belong to the genus *Culicoides*. Sand flies are small enough to pass through the average screen put up to bar mosquitoes. They breed in decaying vegetation and in brackish water, along the edges of pools, and in tree holes. Until such inventions as DDT, people were almost completely helpless against them. The tiny insects fly in swarms, usually at dusk or on overcast days, and attack victims with sharp, stinging bites. They do more than bite. The sand flies of tropical regions transmit dengue fever. This disease, while seldom fatal, produces very high fevers and is so painful that it is commonly called breakbone fever.

Midges can be hard to discourage. An American artist, George F. Mason, tells of his experience while painting in Alaska. He smeared "fly dope" over his face, arms, and hands, but still the midges hovered over him and crept into his eyes and nose. When his canvases were finished, there were countless tiny bumps showing in the paint—corpses of no-see-ums.

Gall Flies

The tiny gall midges are well known because of what they do rather than what they look like. In the air these minute flies are all but invisible. A microscope or strong hand lens reveals that they have transparent, gauzy wings, beaded antennae, and, for such little creatures, long legs.

The name gall fly or gall midge is appropriate because their breeding habits cause little swellings, called *galls*, to develop on plants. Flies are not the only insects that cause galls. Moths, certain wasps, beetles, and aphids also cause them, but Diptera is the largest group involved. Among flies, the majority of gall-makers belong to a single family, *Cecidomyidae*.

More than half of all existing plant families are atacked by gall-producing insects. Galls may be formed in almost any part—stem, root, bud, flower, or leaf —but only if the insect enters while the plant is in the growing stage. Walk in any weed-filled city lot, suburban or country field, and you will find plants with swellings about the size of a good wad of bubble gum located on their stems. Most likely the plants are goldenrod, a plant frequently chosen by a fly that deposits its egg in the stem. This is done during late summer or early fall. The egg soon hatches into a larva that begins to nibble the juicy plant tissue surrounding it. Soon a swelling begins to show on the stem. And considering the size of the fly that is behind the whole project, it grows until it is a globe of amazing size. It is believed that the abnormal growth results from a chemical secretion released by the feeding larva. Inside its snug home, surrounded by

Midge — *Culicoides*

49

plentiful food, the larva grows until it is ready to pupate. The pupa then rests quietly until spring when the adult fly emerges.

A small moth also favors goldenrod for its nursery. The gall it produces is oblong-shaped rather than round. Often two galls, one from the fly and one from the moth, will be seen on a single goldenrod stem. One type of gnat seeks willow trees for its egg-laying. The female lights on a twig and places her egg on the tip of a leaf bud. As the larva eats, the leaf becomes stunted and overlaps around the grub. Gradually a compact, cone-like shelter is created in which the immature fly spends the winter.

Man has little cause to worry about the bumps and lumps created on goldenrods and willows by midges and gnats. There are, however, similar flies, serious pests, that ruin entire crops of wheat, rye, and barley. One of the worst is the Hessian fly. It lays its eggs along the stems of these cultivated grasses and the hatching larvae feed on them. The damage to the stems causes the plants to die. Since there are two or three generations of flies a year, great damage results. Some years, because of their presence, a loss of crops worth close to a million dollars has occurred in the United States.

The Hessian fly is believed to have lived originally in Asia. By some means it spread to Europe, and from there it was carried to America in straw brought along by Hessian soldiers coming to fight in the Revolutionary War. Once in America, the Hessian fly went west with the pioneers. In little more than a hundred years the flies had crossed the entire continent, wheat field by wheat field, as the settlers moved westward.

The story of the Hessian fly is a good example of an ever-present and dangerous problem. Unless the federal and state entomologists are always on the alert, harmful insects may be imported into the country or across state lines. A long list of harmful flies has been imported into the United States. Among them are midges that damage fruit and grain crops, flies that damage trees and timber, and livestock pests. A more serious importation of a two-winged fly occurred some years ago in Brazil.

In March 1930, an African malaria mosquito, never seen before in Brazil, turned up near the seaport of Natal. How it got there nobody knows, but it is a good bet that it came off a French ship from Dakar on the west coast of Africa. A year later the mosquitoes had spread more than one hundred miles up and down the coast. And by 1938 there were so many that they caused a serious epidemic of malaria. Fourteen thousand people died in the first six months. Many more were to succumb, but the mosquitoes were finally wiped out by 1940.

In spite of modern methods of controlling insects, nations must be constantly on guard to prevent unwanted flies from entering their borders. In an age when planes can travel around the world in a few days, the danger of their extending their range is always present and always great.

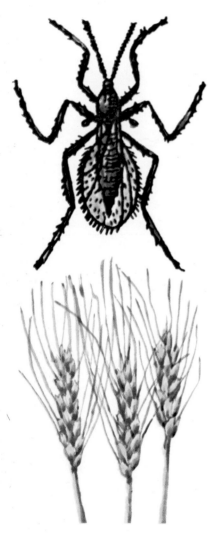

Hessian fly—
Phytophaga destructor

Wheat

Bee fly—
Bombylius major

Look-Alikes

Certain animals—especially insects—might well serve as teachers in the art of disguise, for theiy have successfully become "carbon copies" of others. Animals that look like other animals are called mimics. Among insects that have developed mimicry are many Diptera—bee flies, flower flies, and robber flies.

Why should one animal look like another? What purpose does it serve? How does it happen? By accident? By some mysterious force? These questions have been debated by scientists for a number of years. There are many ideas about mimics, but little agreement. Most widely accepted is a theory called Batesian mimicry, named for the English naturalist Bates, who first suggested it. It proposes that an insect without powers of self-defense is protected from its enemies because it looks like another which does have means of protection such as a stinger or poisonous secretion. Another idea is that the mimic may be able to take advantage of another insect's home because it is not detected as an invader.

A mimic that you are likely to see on sunny summer days is the bee fly. It may be hovering close to the ground over city pavements or a woodland path. Its vibrating wings produce a noisy bee-like buzz. Its fuzzy abdomen is covered with short, thickly set hairs, yellow or orange, black or white, or a combination of several colors. The transparent wings are marked with black blotches. You might easily mistake it for a bumblebee.

51

Two thousand species of bee flies have been recorded. One of the most common is *Bombylius major*, a large insect densely covered with white, brown, and black hairs. It is at home practically everywhere in the northern hemisphere, appearing in late spring and remaining active for only a couple of months. The adult dines on flower nectar, but the larvae need a different diet. As soon as they hatch they begin hunting for a bumblebee nest or for another suitable home. Usually they do not have far to go, because the female bee fly hovers over entrances of a real bee nest and sprays it with her tiny eggs.

The tiny, spiny maggot works its way into a bee's nest and settles down in the waxen cell the female bee has prepared for her own offspring. At first the fly maggot feeds on the pollen or honey stored for the use of the bee larvae, but soon it attacks the larval bee and sucks the contents of the young bee into its own body.

Besides the bee larvae, the maggots of the family *Bombyliidae* attack a variety of homes and hosts. Among the hosts are caterpillars, grasshopper eggs, and beetle grubs. In Africa several species of bee flies are parasites on the pupae of tsetse flies. Thus they reduce, at least to a small extent, the numbers of these disease carriers.

One of the syrphids—the yellow and black drone fly—bears a strong resemblance to the male, or drone, honeybee. The larvae of this species flourish in vegetable debris and manure heaps. They also develop in decaying flesh, and this fact was responsible for an odd myth in ancient times: People had noted swarms of the yellow and black drone flies emerging from rotting carcasses, and concluded that bees spring to life in the bodies of dead animals.

Some robber flies resemble bees so closely that they can successfully attack the adult insects they resemble. There is one North American species with a rounded abdomen with a thick covering of hair, most often gold and black in color, very similar to many bees. Like all robber flies it preys on flying insects. Small bumblebees, wasps, and honeybees, despite their stingers, are at its mercy. The resemblance of the fly to bees may help it get close to unsuspecting prey, but this is a theory that still must be proved.

In India and Africa there are robber flies that copy big carpenter bees. Not only do the flies resemble the bees in size, shape, and color, but they choose the same trees, stems, or fences in which to burrow and lay their eggs. The adult flies prey upon the look-alike bees, and also on other insects. Probably the flies have the benefit of some protection from enemies that would not hesitate to attack a fly, but would stay clear of a stinger-equipped bee. The robber fly larvae, like the larvae of bee flies, work their way into the burrows of bees. They not only devour any dead pupae they find, but they suck dry the living larvae.

Two other look-alike flies worth mentioning are those that resemble wasps and moths. Members of the family *Conopidae* have a nipped-in "waist" and wasp-like coloring.

The moth fly resembles the moth in the shape of its body, wings, and legs. Even the antennae are covered with fine hairs, increasing the moth resemblance. This fly is such a small insect that it might go quite unnoticed except for its preference for house windows. It walks endlessly back and forth on them, spreading and folding its wings as it goes.

Mimicry must not be interpreted to mean that the look-alike knows what it is doing, or that the bee flies, for example, deliberately set out to look like their victims. More likely in some far-off time there was an ancestor of the bee fly that may already have been feeding on bee larvae. In the course of time a gene change occurred producing offspring that looked a little more like bees. This gave them a better chance to feed, survive, and breed. Their descendants resembled bees to an even greater extent, and in time a new species developed.

The resemblance of one animal to another is probably a matter of chance variations that may help in survival. Just as many mutations occur that are harmful, that decrease the chances of surviving and having offspring. Thus through a process called *natural selection* animals that are able to feed and breed successfully may become a new species. Those that cannot, die away.

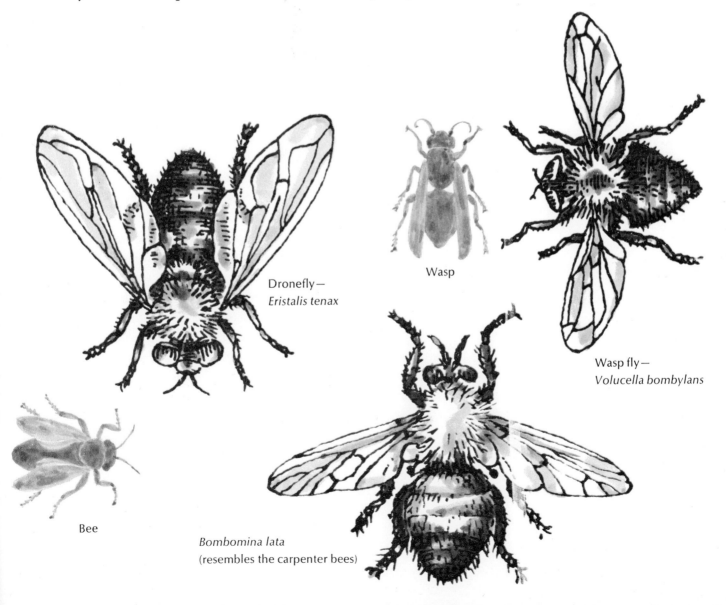

Dronefly—
Eristalis tenax

Wasp

Wasp fly—
Volucella bombylans

Bee

Bombomina lata
(resembles the carpenter bees)

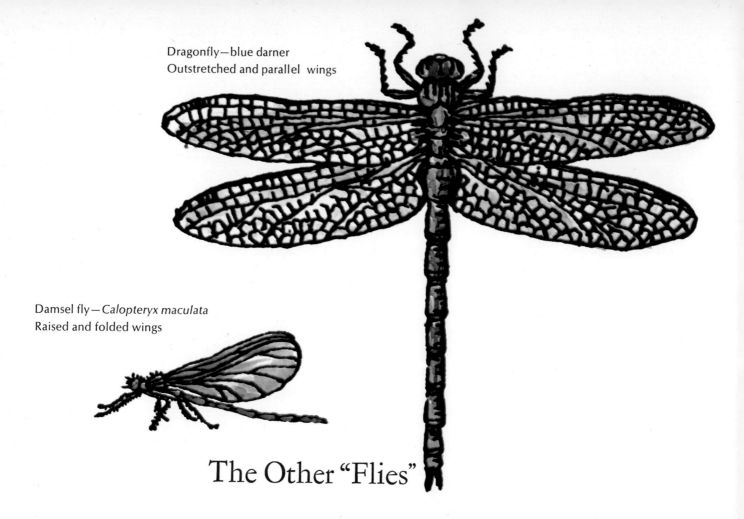

Dragonfly—blue darner
Outstretched and parallel wings

Damsel fly—*Calopteryx maculata*
Raised and folded wings

The Other "Flies"

No one is likely to think of butterflies as being closely related to the Diptera. Because of their large, showy wings, they are outstandingly themselves. But there are a number of other insects that people are often not sure about. Is the mayfly a "true" fly? And what about fireflies and dragonflies? None belong with the Diptera. They—and other insects popularly called flies—are members of other orders.

Dragonflies have a variety of popular names including mosquito hawks, bee butchers, darning needles, and horse stingers. Some of these rather dangerous-sounding names are the result of superstitions. Darning needle, for instance, is based on the myth that these insects sew up the ears of truant schoolchildren. They can't sting horses because they do not have stingers.

The name mosquito hawk is well earned. Dragonflies feed on mosquitoes and other prey they seize in flight. Their long, slender legs outlined with stiff bristles are held forward on a slant, forming a scoop net. The victims are caught in these traps and held until the dragonfly settles on a perch where it devours them at leisure.

A dragonfly's wings are of interest for several reasons. There are two pairs (not a single pair as in the Diptera) and each pair moves independently of the other. Most four-winged insects move the front and hind pairs together. The dragonfly sets its stroke by putting the hind wings in motion first and flies with

54

each pair moving out of step. Since speed of flight depends upon the number of times wings "bite" into the air, this operation is most successful. Dragonflies travel swiftly—at speeds up to thirty miles an hour, occasionally faster. A house fly, speedy as it may appear, is not likely to achieve more than four miles an hour.

Dragonflies and their close relatives, the damselflies, form the order Odonata. Members of the order have long, straight abdomens, two pairs of thickly veined wings, and large, compound eyes. There is great variation in their size, depending on the species. In the tropics damselflies tend to be very large; in North America they are small. Dragonflies in North America are larger and stronger fliers than the damselflies. One way of telling the two groups apart is by the position of the wings when at rest. Dragonflies hold theirs outstretched. Damselflies hold the wings together above the body.

Both are a great aid to humans in destroying mosquitoes and other pests. The adults catch and eat adult mosquitoes. The larvae of both dragonflies and damselflies devour countless mosquito larvae. Their appetites are enormous. One adult kept under observation ate forty house flies within two hours. The pesky deer flies are also prominent in the dragonfly menu and these large, elegant insects are often found hunting in woods far from the nearest water.

Dragonflies and damselflies are truly ancient insects. In prehistoric times they flew through the lush vegetation that would later form great beds of coal. Along with the fossil plants in coal beds, fossil impressions of dragonfly ancestors have been found with wingspreads of twenty-nine inches. (Today the largest known dragonfly has a wingspread of five inches.) It is not known whether ancestors of mosquitoes also existed in those days. Possibly the forerunners of the dragonflies fed on cockroaches.

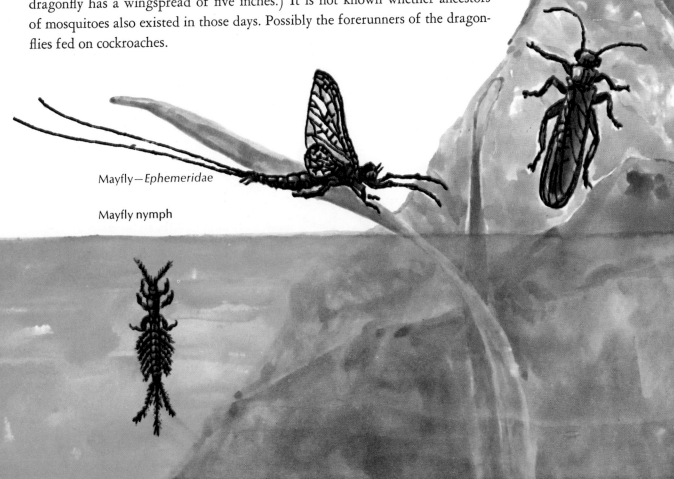

Stonefly—
Plecoptera

Mayfly—*Ephemeridae*

Mayfly nymph

Today about five thousand known species of Odonata live in all parts of the world. Probably best known in the United States is the green darner (*Anax junius*), a handsome insect, with shining, olive-green thorax and a brown, blue-trimmed abdomen.

Food for Fish

Flies and other insects are an important source of food for fish, none more so than the mayflies. Without these delicate insects freshwater fish would be reduced in an alarming fashion. Mayflies are found in the vicinity of ponds and lakes and along streams, for the young hatch and develop in water. In fact most of the mayfly's life is spent in water. The adults usually live only a few hours, just long enough to mate and lay eggs.

When the long aquatic phase is finished, the adults emerge in great swarms. In cities and towns bordering the Great Lakes they sometimes appear in such numbers as to suggest a sleet storm. For several days one group after another emerges. They are a great nuisance, covering windows.

The adult males and females mate in a peculiar, graceful, and measured bobbing flight called the "mating dance." Great numbers die, but many return to the nearby lakes. The females drop their eggs in clusters of hundreds of eggs. Those that reach water sink to the bottom and soon hatch into little fringed larvae known as naiads. The fringes are gills.

Naiads require from several weeks to several months and go through a number of molts before developing into the adult stage, depending on the species. When the naiads have passed through all their stages and are fully grown, they come to the water's surface. They molt one last time and adults emerge. They fly a short distance, then rest. In a few hours they molt once more. Mayflies are the only insects that molt after developing wings.

After the adult molt the mayflies emerge, delicate and shining, ready to fly on gauze-like wings. Their flights and their lives are brief indeed, however. An adult may live only a few hours, and never more than two or three days. The name of their order is Ephemerida, taken from the Greek word for "day."

Caddisfly fishing net

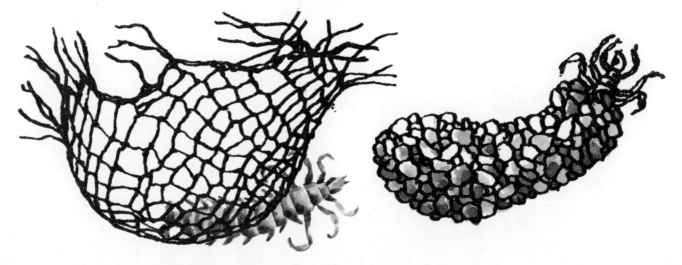

Stoneflies, like mayflies, are a tremendous source of food for freshwater fish such as trout and bass. If you explore rocks or large stones in a fast-moving stream, you are quite certain to find stonefly naiads on the damp surfaces. Stoneflies are found only in temperate regions and seem to thrive in cool water. One species stops growing in summer, resumes in fall, and becomes adult between early January and the end of March and crawls about on the snow.

Like mayflies, the stoneflies (order Plecoptera) have a short adult life—many of them do not eat. Although they are weak fliers, like the mayflies, they do travel a distance for their mating. And the brief span is enough for a female to produce between five thousand and six thousand eggs, each about the size of a pin point. Adults measure from as little as half an inch to two inches in length. Stoneflies are attracted by light, and large numbers of them may be seen on warm summer evenings flying around street lamps, or clinging to them. Fishermen not only use adults and naiads for bait, but they copy the adults in man-made "flies" to use as lures.

More "Flies" in Name Only

Caddisfly is the name given to the moth-like insects of the order Trichoptera. Although caddisflies resemble moths at first glance, a more careful look shows many differences. For one thing, their wings are usually without the bright patterns of color that make moths so attractive. The adults have larger antennae than moths, and mouth parts that are suited for lapping rather than the coiled, sucking mouths of moths.

Caddisfly—
Trichoptera

The most interesting thing about caddisflies, however, is their aquatic larvae. They live in all kinds of freshwater and typically each one builds a little house of sand, small pebbles, shells, or bits of vegetation held together with silk.

Each house is so distinctive that the various species can be told apart simply by their cases. Some caddisfly cases look like tiny ice-cream cones, others look like snail shells. Then there is a stagnant water species that builds a case of grass stems stacked together so that the completed case looks quite a bit like a log cabin. The silk for case building is produced as needed in the body, and pours

Types of caddisfly larva cases

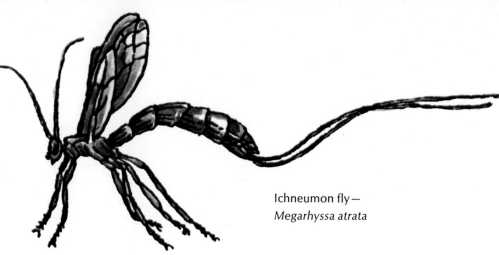

Ichneumon fly—
Megarhyssa atrata

Ichneumon
drilling hole
in wood wasp
larva.

out of the little insect's mouth. In the water it hardens. The caddisfly larva assembles its materials with great care, fitting pieces of stone or sand neatly against each other and "gluing" them with the silk.

A few caddis worms, as the larvae are called, do not build protective cases, but they may spin silken tubes as a covering. Silk is also used to make a little fishing net that caddis fly larvae use to catch the tiny water creatures they eat.

One of the largest and most important orders of insects is the order Hymenoptera. It contains the ants, bees, and wasps. Two familiar members of the order Hymenoptera are commonly called flies—the sawflies and ichneumon flies.

The female sawfly has an ovipositor or egg-laying organ made of two flat, pointed, and saw-toothed plates at the tip of her abdomen. By moving these plates in opposite directions she can slit a leaf or stem so that an egg may be inserted in it. These are the "saws" that give this insect its popular name. Among the species found commonly in the United States are the elm sawfly, the pine sawfly, and wheat-stem sawfly. Each gets its name from the plant on which it lays its eggs—and each is a severe pest.

While these insects belong to the order of bees and wasps and are called flies, their larvae look like caterpillars and resemble the larvae of butterflies and moths. Sawfly larvae have legs and can move around from place to place. Some of them can also give off stinking fluids that drive away birds.

The ichnuemon flies look like wasps with a sting long enough to go right through a finger. Fortunately the long organ that trails so threateningly is not a stinger but an egg layer. Like its cousin the sawfly, the female ichnuemon uses her ovipositor to drill into the place where she lays her egg. Unlike the sawfly, the ichnuemon always lays her eggs on some other insect; often the insect parasitized is the sawfly. It is not exaggerating to call ichneumon flies hereditary enemies of sawflies.

Fireflies or lightning bugs are not true flies nor are they bugs (order Hemiptera). They are beetles, one family of the enormous order Coleoptera. Anyone who has ever seen the flashes of greenish-yellow light in the dark of a summer's evening will agree that the name firefly well suits these attractive insects.

58

The light made by fireflies delighted and puzzled people for many years before they were able to understand much about it. How was it produced? What was its purpose? How was it turned on and off? What was the secret of this light that had almost no heat? Many scientists had tried to produce "cold light," but none had succeeded.

Today most questions about fireflies have been answered. The light is created in segments of the abdomen where the tissues produce two chemicals. One is the chemical that gives off light, and the other sets the first in action. But before the two chemicals can react oxygen is needed.

In the tissues, also, are little tubes—as thin as thread—through which air can pass. The air brings in oxygen, which makes possible the chemical reaction. Light results.

The light of fireflies apparently serves to bring opposite sexes together for mating. The light-up segments are the last several of the abdomens of males; on the females the light may be limited to a single segment. In some species the females are without wings and spend their entire lives on the ground. This does not prevent their shining in the dark, however. They are known as glowworms.

The turning on and off of light seems to result from nerves that regulate the amount of oxygen entering the light-up tissues.

After solving the mystery of cold light, scientists are anxious to use it as a tool in investigating the effects of drugs, heat, and cold on living things. The cost of creating the living light, which fireflies turn on and off as easily as we take a breath, is so tremendous, however, that any large-scale production is impractical. Cold light, with all its beauty and intrigue, still belongs to the insects.

Fireflies—
Lampyridae

Index

DOROTHY SHUTTLESWORTH has been exploring nature since she started working for The American Museum of Natural History in New York at the age of seventeen. After several years there on the staff of *Natural History*, she became the first editor of a similar magazine for young people, *Junior Natural History*. She held the position for twelve years.

Although in recent years she has been occupied more as a homemaker than as a writer, she has authored more than a dozen books on nature and science as well as many magazine articles. Mrs. Shuttlesworth lives in East Orange, New Jersey, with her husband, who is a high school principal. Her son has recently married and her daughter is a student at the University of Kentucky.

BARBARA WOLFF is a native-born New Yorker. She attended Hunter College, where she received an A.B. in art. She has taught elementary school, worked in the art department of a major periodical, and has worked for a professional designer. At present she does freelance illustration and still lives in New York, where her husband is an art director for an advertising agency.